MICHAEL J. FOX

A Little Golden Book® Biography

By Lori Haskins Houran
Illustrated by Giovanni Abeille

 A GOLDEN BOOK • NEW YORK

Once, there was a very small kid who grew up to be a very big star!

Michael Fox was born on June 9, 1961, in Edmonton, Canada.

He was always small for his age. When Michael was six, people thought his three-year-old sister was his twin.

He was the shortest kid in his class, year after year.

Michael's favorite sport was hockey, but his size made him easy to knock around. His parents were constantly taking him to get stitches!

Luckily, Michael found a new passion: acting.

It turned out he had a special talent for making people laugh. He could crack up a whole audience just by the way he said something or the look on his face.

Michael loved that feeling! He joined every play his school put on.

In 1977, Michael's teacher told him about an audition. A TV show called *Leo & Me* needed someone to play Jamie, a funny twelve-year-old who lives on a yacht with his uncle Leo.

Why not try out? Michael was sixteen, but he *looked* twelve.

Sure enough, Michael got the part. For once, his height had helped him out!

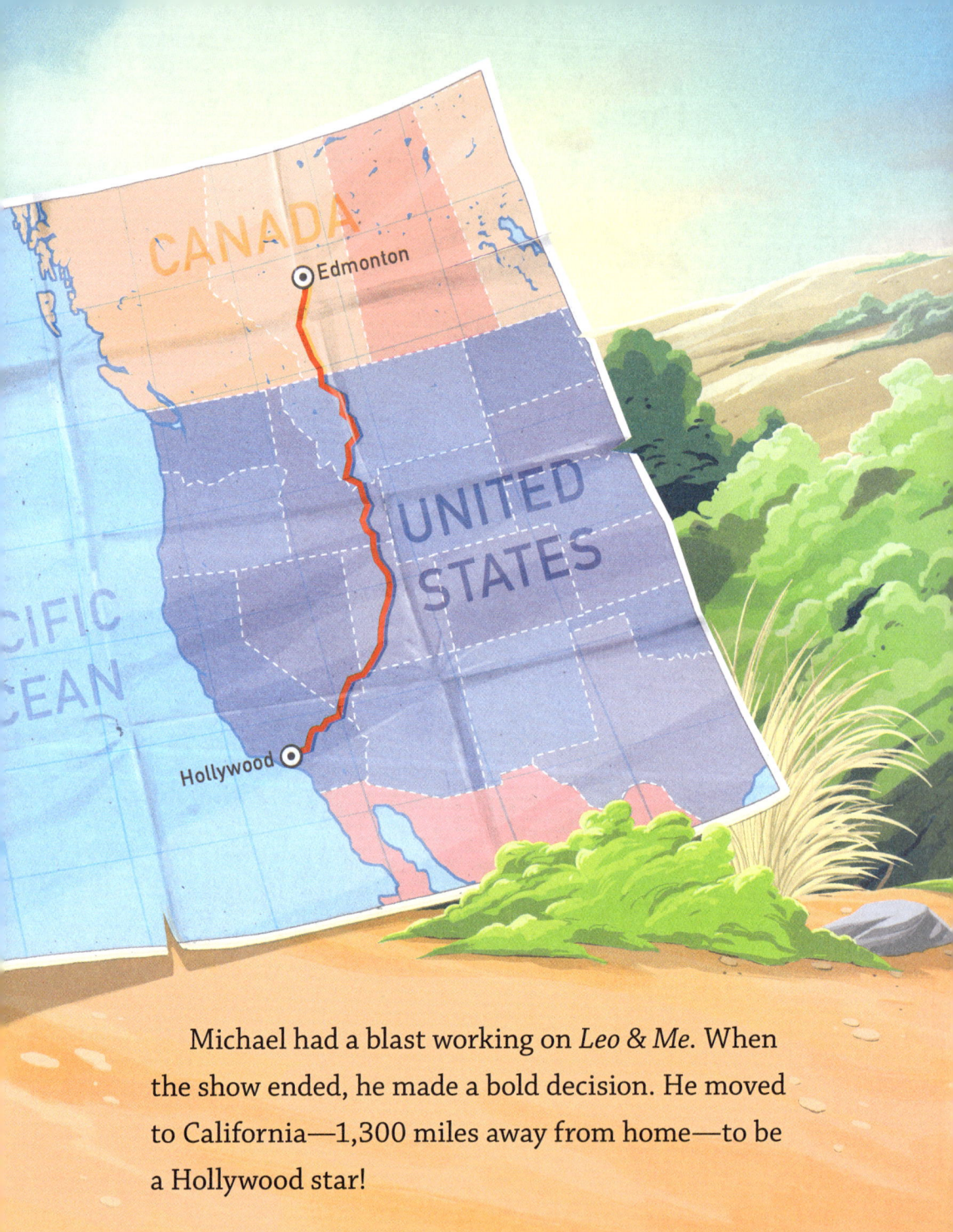

Michael had a blast working on *Leo & Me*. When the show ended, he made a bold decision. He moved to California—1,300 miles away from home—to be a Hollywood star!

Just one problem—there was already an actor there named Michael Fox.

Michael's middle name is Andrew. He thought about calling himself "Michael A. Fox," but it didn't sound right. So he picked a different letter and became Michael J. Fox.

Michael found lots of acting jobs in Hollywood, but they were small parts that didn't pay much.

After three years, he was out of money. He had to sell his furniture to buy food! Maybe it was time to give up on his dream and go home.

Then Michael got great news. He had won a part—a big part—on a TV show called *Family Ties*.

Just like before, Michael would play someone younger than him. He was twenty-one years old, but his character, Alex P. Keaton, was sixteen.

Could he pull it off?

YES!

The show was an instant hit. Viewers adored Alex, and the charming actor who brought him to life.

Michael quickly got offered another teenage part— this time in a movie! He played Scott Howard, a high school basketball player who turns into a werewolf, in *Teen Wolf.*

Then came the movie that changed Michael's life forever.

In 1985, Michael starred in *Back to the Future* as Marty McFly, a typical teen who skateboards, plays guitar . . . and accidentally travels through time!

Marty ends up in the year 1955, where he meets his parents when *they* were teenagers. He helps his dad stand up to a bully and win his mom's heart.

Back to the Future was the top movie of the year and is one of the most popular movies ever!

Suddenly, Michael was a superstar!

Fans wanted his autograph. Magazines rushed to put his face on their covers. Movie roles came pouring in.

Meanwhile, back on his show *Family Ties,* Michael's character, Alex, fell in love. His girlfriend was played by actress Tracy Pollan.

In real life, Michael fell in love with Tracy, too! They got married in 1988 and started a family.

Everything was going Michael's way.

"When the cure for Parkinson's is found—and it will be—it will be because of all of us, working together."

Then, one morning, Michael noticed something strange. His left pinky finger was shaking, and he couldn't make it stop.

Michael went to the doctor. He was stunned to learn that he had a disease called Parkinson's. Over time, it causes serious health problems.

At first, Michael kept his illness private. But in
2000, he started the Michael J. Fox Foundation for
Parkinson's Research.

The foundation has raised over two *billion* dollars!

Michael kept on acting until 2021. He appeared in dozens of TV shows and movies, including two *Back to the Future* sequels.

One special role? Playing the voice of Stuart Little in three films. Michael had a lot in common with Stuart, a small mouse who goes on big adventures!

Michael won many awards and honors over the years, including five Emmys, four Golden Globes, and a star on the Hollywood Walk of Fame.

"It's a great thing . . . to do something you love," Michael said, "and to hear that maybe you've done something to make people happy."

In 2022, Michael received a special Oscar for his work supporting Parkinson's research. When his name was called at the Academy Awards ceremony, the audience gave him a standing ovation.

Thanks to his talent and generosity, Michael J. Fox became one of the best-loved actors of all time. And he will be . . .

. . . far into the **FUTURE**.